PowerKids Readers:
Nature Books™

Rivers

Jacqueline Dwyer

The Rosen Publishing Group's
PowerKids Press™
New York

1

Published in 2001 by The Rosen Publishing Group, Inc.
29 East 21st Street, New York, NY 10010

First Edition

Book Design: Michael de Guzman
Layout: Felicity Erwin and Edwin Yoo

Photo Credits: p. 1 © F.P.G./Alan Kearney; p. 5 © Earth Scenes/Ronald Toms, OSF; p. 7 © International Stock/Wayne Aldridge; p. 9 © F.P.G./Josef Beck; p. 11 © Earth Scenes/Maria Zorn; p. 13 © CORBIS/John Watkins, Frank Lane Picture Agency; p. 15 © Earth Scenes/David Welling; p. 17 © F.P.G./Lee Foster; pp. 19, 21 © F.P.G./Ron Chapple; p. 22 (stream) © Earth Scenes/John Lemker.

Dwyer, Jacqueline.
    Rivers / by Jacqueline Dwyer.
        p. cm — (PowerKids readers. Nature books)
    Summary: Briefly discusses the characteristics of rivers and the people and animals that live near them.
    Includes index.
    ISBN 0-8239-5681-4 (lib. bdg. : alk. paper)
        1. Rivers—Juvenile literature. [1. Rivers.] I. Title. II. Series.

GB 1203.8 .D98 2000
551.48'3—dc21

                                                    99-058355

Manufactured in the United States of America

Contents

1 Streams of Water 4

2 The Longest River 8

3 Words to Know 22

4 Books and Web Sites 23

5 Index 24

6 Word Count 24

7 Note 24

Rivers are big streams of water.

This tree is at a river's source. The source is the place where a river begins. A river can have a lake as its source.

There are rivers all over the world. The Nile river is the longest river in the world. It is about 4,160 miles (6,695 km) long!

Many plants grow in rivers. The marsh marigold is a plant that grows in rivers.

11

Lots of animals live near rivers, too. The otter is an animal that lives near rivers.

Some rivers have a waterfall. Angel Falls is the highest waterfall in the world.

15

Some rivers are made of ice. A river of ice is called a glacier.

17

People build bridges to cross rivers. The bridge goes from one side of the river to the other.

It is fun to ride in a boat
on a river.

Words to Know

BRIDGE   GLACIER

LAKE   OTTER   PLANT

  STREAM   WATERFALL

Here are more books to read about rivers:
Wonders of Rivers
by Rae Bains
Troll Associates

Let's Explore a River
(Books for Young Explorers)
by Jane R. McCauley
National Geographic Society

To learn more about rivers, check out this
Web site:
http://riverresource.com/text/infolink.html

Index

A
Angel Falls, 14

B
boat, 20
bridge, 18

G
glacier, 16

L
lake, 6

O
otter, 12

N
Nile river, 8

P
plant, 10

S
source, 6
stream, 4

W
waterfall, 14

Word Count: 136

Note to Librarians, Teachers, and Parents

PowerKids Readers (Nature Books) are specially designed to help emergent and beginning readers build their skills in reading for information. Simple vocabulary and concepts are paired with photographs of real kids in real-life situations or stunning, detailed images from the natural world around them. Readers will respond to written language by linking meaning with their own everyday experiences and observations. Sentences are short and simple, employing a basic vocabulary of sight words, as well as new words that describe objects or processes that take place in the natural world. Large type, clean design, and photographs corresponding directly to the text all help children to decipher meaning. Features such as a contents page, picture glossary, and index help children get the most out of PowerKids Readers. They also introduce children to the basic elements of a book, which they will encounter in their future reading experiences. Lists of related books and Web sites encourage kids to explore other sources and to continue the process of learning.